POCKET IMAGES

Honiton & the Otter Valley

This scene epitomizes Honiton and the Otter valley in its combination of the street of the town with the cattle of the countryside. The wet pavements also draw attention to the plentiful rain of the area which ensures the fertile green pastures. This fertility led Thomas Westcote, writing in 1630, to observe of Honiton: 'their Saturday's market, for all kind of victuals, fowl, fruit and corn, is accounted next to the best in this country'.

POCKET IMAGES

Honiton & the Otter Valley

Dr John Yallop, OBE

First published 1992
This new pocket edition 2007
Images unchanged from first edition

Nonsuch Publishing Limited
Cirencester Road, Chalford
Stroud, Gloucestershire, GL6 8PE
www.nonsuch-publishing.com

Nonsuch Publishing is an imprint of NPI Media Group

British Library Cataloguing in Publication Data.
A catalogue record for this book is available from the British Library.

ISBN 978-1-84588-453-6

Typesetting and origination by NPI Media Group
Printed in Great Britain

Contents

Introduction

Many travellers over the last 450 years have recorded impressions of Honiton and the Otter valley. Moving westwards along the Great South West Highway they have been greeted with a scene at the top of Honiton Hill which has moved them at times to well-nigh poetical expression. Defoe (1724) wrote 'Honiton ... may pass not only for a pleasant good town ... but stands in the best and pleasantest part of the whole county, and I cannot but recommend it to any gentlemen that travel this road, that if they please to observe the prospect for half a mile till their coming down the hill and to the entrance into Honiton, the view of the country is the most beautiful landscape in the world–a mere picture–and I do not remember the like in any place in England.' Brice (1759) wrote 'Honiton ... is sit. in one of the best and most pleasant Parts of the County, abounding with Corn and Pasture, and, having a view of the adjacent Country, 1 of the most beautiful of Landscapes', while *The Complete English Traveller* (1790) states of Honiton: 'Before we leave this town, we must not forget to acquaint the reader, that its situation is not only the most beautiful in England, but even exceeds imagination. It stands in the most delightful part of the county, the fields around are cultivated with so much industry, and the prospect from the town so inchanting, that it would require the pencil of Raphael to display all its perfections.' Such eulogies continued and we find Burrit (1865) observing: 'The valley you look down upon, as you descend into Honiton ... is one of the most beautiful in England', while Gould (1899) urged that 'One thing no visitor should fail to see, and that is the superb view from Honiton Hill.'

The impressions of the town itself tend to emphasize its position on the highway. The earliest is by Leland (1534–43), who wrote 'Honiton is a fair long thorough Fare and Market Toun', while Hooker (1599), in the earliest history of Devon, described it as '... a faire Towne livinge for suche as be bounden to and from London and therefore it hath the more Innes in it'. Others who give similar descriptions include *The English Traveller* (1746): 'This Town is a large Thoroughfare, and consists principally of a long Street'; Moule (1837): 'It consists principally of one broad Street, through which passes the road from Chard to Exeter', and Stawell (1910): '... the straight wide street of Honiton'.

The reasons for these consistent views may be found in the history of Honiton and the valley. The Blackdown region, which stretches from the Vale of Taunton to the Channel coast, consists of a dissected plateau, that is a flat upland area from which water-flows have carved valleys. The major one is the Otter valley, which emerges to the west and has thus become the chief channel in the area for east–west travel. The Roman road engineers exploited this geography when constructing a road from Dorchester to Exeter and it is of interest to note that the nineteenth-century railway engineers, who were unlikely to have been familiar with the work of their predecessors, arrived at the same solution to the problem of traversing this stretch of country. The Saxon conquest and settlement give us the first reference to Honiton by name, but it was merely one of numerous small manors in the Otter valley. A big change occurred around 1200 when William de Vernon, the lord of the manor, followed a common practice of the time and created a new town. The old manor was in the area where St Michael's church now stands, but the new town was placed astride the main highway, the former Roman road. The plan was strictly geometrical and survived almost unaltered into the twentieth century, as may be seen in Section Six, Honiton From The Air.

New towns were set up with the object of encouraging trade and Honiton did this on account of its position on a great highway. As a result it became the premier place in the Otter valley, acting as the market centre for the surrounding area. The building of Bishop Grandisson's magnificent church at Ottery St Mary might have produced a rival centre but it did not, since Ottery did not possess the potential for trade which was Honiton's great strength.

Much of this history lies before the age of photography and thus outside the scope of this book. Nevertheless, Honiton and the Otter valley are as they are because of this history, and photographic records covering approximately the century 1850 to 1950 reflect this in many ways. Pictures of the Otter valley illustrate both the geological structure of the countryside and, even without the modern advantage of colour, enable us to share something of the excitement so obviously felt by many travellers when the view from Honiton Hill burst upon their sight. Many of the village photographs show that the beauty observable on the broad view is just as much present on close and more detailed inspection.

The travellers' impression of a great thoroughfare and a principal broad street is abundantly conveyed in the pictures of Honiton High Street, and the connection between the old settlement and the new town comes to life in the views of New Street and Church Hill. The purpose of the new town was to encourage trade and this aspect is illustrated in the section on markets and industries. Neither towns nor villages would exist without people and the many seen in these photographs may be regarded, in principle, as the descendants of those who greeted King Henry III in 1230, Lord Russel in 1549, King Charles I in 1643, the Prince of Orange in 1688, the first railway train in 1860 and who inspected the ruins of St Michael's church in 1911.

Honiton was fortunate in having William Edward Heath as a resident of the town. In *Kelly's Directory* for 1856 he is listed as a photographic artist and in *Billin's Directory* for 1857 as that combined with being manager of the gas works and an insurance agent. In Allhallows Museum photographic collection there are a number of photographs, some of which are reproduced in this book, which depict aspects of the town at this period, for example the street decorations of 1856 and the building of the railway 1859/60. There is no proof that these are Heath's work, but since they are contemporary with his presence in the town and no other photographs are known earlier than about 1880 it seems probable that they are his. The next known professional photographer was Alfred John Griffiths, who was active from 1883 to 1919 and was responsible, in particular, for the portraits shown on pages 118 and 119.

One aspect of the town and area may seem to have been less than adequately covered. For many centuries Honiton was an important textile centre, being the third cloth town in Devon in medieval times. However, the industry had died out before the age of photography. The lace industry, whose principal and original centre was Honiton, but which extended to most of the villages in East Devon, did survive into the photographic era but relics are for the most part pieces of lace. A few photographs have been included and more will be found in my book *The History of the Honiton Lace Industry*.

I did consider the inclusion of a 'then and now' section but decided that a better approach was to invite readers to take the book for a walk around and endeavour to compare the pictures with the same scene today from the same viewpoint–traffic permitting! It will be found that in many cases there has been very little change, even in the town scenes, provided, in the latter case, one allows for the modern proliferation of street furniture. In places where appreciable change has taken place it has, on the whole, not been disastrous–with the notable exception of the railway station. It is to be hoped that books such as this may contribute to an awareness which could prevent insensitive treatment of our towns and villages.

One

The Otter Valley

The two things with which the Otter valley is, perhaps, most associated are the town of Honiton and the hill of Dumpdon. This picture introduces the valley by showing both.

The upper photograph, which in fact dates from the early twentieth century, is a virtually timeless impression of the Otter valley with its fields separated by Devon hedgebanks climbing up the sides. The lower photograph would likewise be timeless were it not for the Royal Blue coach on its way to London in competition with the train.

The eastern half of East Devon constitutes the area known as the Blackdown Hills and many people are misled into supposing it to be a region of hills and valleys. This is not so, for the area constitutes what is known geologically as a dissected plateau: a flat-topped upland in which water erosion has carved out valleys. So in East Devon there are valleys carved out by rivers such as the Otter, the Culm, the Sid, the Coly and others, but the land between is flat. It is therefore possible to travel considerable distances in East Devon without going appreciably up or down hill. One may, for example, travel from the vicinity of Ottery St Mary to the Wellington Monument, a distance of some twenty-five miles, and remain at between 700 and 900 feet above sea level. The evidence for this is very well shown in this early twentieth-century view over Honiton from the south, for the top of the 'hills' to the north is a straight horizontal line.

Although the hill of Dumpdon, crowned with its clump of beech trees and Iron Age rampart, is the most striking aspect of the Otter valley, the hill of St Cyres is perhaps the most beautiful. It forms a marvellous backdrop to many views in Honiton and to the town as a whole when seen from the south. Its woods were plentifully inhabited by red squirrels within living memory. In 1936 it was the foreground to a marvellous display of the Aurora Borealis, never to be forgotten by those who saw it.

Though there are many fields with Devon hedgebanks, the Otter valley is also well wooded. The extent of the woods on St Cyres is shown in the upper picture where the whole hill and Tracey House are swathed in trees. At higher levels, above the greensand, the geology favours beech and above Honiton, in the direction of Gittisham, there is Beech Walk, shown below. These views are little changed.

The central feature of the valley is the River Otter, seen here peacefully flowing past St Cyres above and Dumpdon below. The main change in the river does not show in the photographs: an increase in pollution which has had a serious effect on the trout population. Efforts are now being made to rectify this state of affairs but damage is liable to take much longer to repair than it was to cause.

The river scene was not always so pastorally serene as the pictures on the previous page suggest. On 11 January 1913, for example, there were extensive floods. The wall to the right is, in fact, the upper part of Clapper Bridge on the Honiton to Combe Raleigh road. The arches are submerged but the road is clear enough for the lady and gentleman to walk across it. Not only has the river overflowed its banks but there are temporary ponds and lakes in the fields.

The road from Honiton to Combe Raleigh is seen here from Clapper Bridge during the floods of 11 January 1913. The high axles of the vehicles and the long legs of the horses meant that the road was passable as it would not have been to modern motor vehicles other than tractors. The nearside wheel of the oncoming vehicle appears to be at a strange angle, as though about to part company with the axle: we can only hope that it didn't.

From source to sea the River Otter is crossed by nineteen bridges, the principal ones bearing names. A typical example is Langford Bridge on the Honiton to Dunkeswell road, seen here in about 1930. In the intervening decades little has changed and a photograph taken from the same position today would be virtually indistinguishable from this. Scenes such as this have entranced travellers for centuries but none has expressed his feelings more clearly than the American E. Burritt. In his 1865 book, *A Walk from London to Land's End and Back*, he wrote: 'The valley you look down upon, as you descend into Honiton from the north is one of the most beautiful in England. Right in the centre of it apparently arises Dumpdon, a remarkable hill panelled to the crown with those infinitely-varied patches of verdure and red soil. The name seems to suggest a down "dumped" bolt upright in the middle of the great valley.'

Unlike Langford Bridge, Tracey Bridge (OS = Stoneyford), on the Honiton to Awliscombe road, has been swept away in favour of a wider bridge to cater for increased traffic flow.

Some country houses have been engulfed by the expansion of Honiton so Oakmount, seen here in splendid isolation, is now surrounded by a widened road, the bypass and the British Legion Hall.

This pre-mechanization scene brings to life the old song which includes the line 'four men went to mow: went to mow a meadow'—only the dog is missing, but one may suspect he is lurking somewhere ready to intercept any bolting rabbits. It is fascinating to watch an expert scythesman at work, with his even rhythmic action. It is, however, essential to keep the blade razor sharp, so there are frequent stops, as here, to hone the blade. The hone stones used by these men were in all probability local products from the Dunkeswell area, whose considerable output supplied not only local requirements but even an export trade from Exeter quay.

Although the number of sheep in Devon has declined from the great days of the medieval cloth industry, they are by no means extinct and a wide variety are to be seen at the annual Honiton Show, held on the first Thursday in August. This event—one of the main features of the Otter valley's year—has been staged for over a century and is the largest one-day show in the South-West. The picture depicts sheep 'posing' for their photographs in the show pens in the 1930s. Various familiar features of the show may be seen, including the bowler hat, stick and ubiquitous binder twine, without which farming, seemingly, would be impossible.

Two

Honiton Around the Town

Most people's impression of Honiton is that it consists of one long straight street, typified by this 1930s photograph. The policeman on point duty is now a thing of the past. The soldier talking to him is CSM Harry Agger, the Allhallows School instructor, groundsman and general guide, philosopher and friend to generations of boys.

At the beginning of the twentieth century Honiton had scarcely expanded beyond its medieval boundaries and there were still only two houses in Kings Road.

There was, however, some expansion eastwards along the London road in the development known as East End.

Opposite East End stands Holyshute House, a nineteenth-century property built above the Holyshute spring. The waters were said to have medicinal virtues and were probably the source of the pool in which the 'Honiton Hippos' drowned 100,000 years ago. Their bones were found when the bypass was built.

Marwood House, a little to the west of Holyshute, is Honiton's oldest surviving private house, dating from 1617. It was built for John Marwood, the son of Queen Elizabeth's physician. King Charles I stayed here in 1644.

There was once a competition for the world's most boring postcard. Surely this view of the eastern end of the High Street, devoid of people, animals or vehicles, could well have won a prize?

This more animated scene is notable for showing Honiton's first Devonia cinema on the right. The board outside advertises the week's attraction as *Dancing on the Vicarage Lawn*—a far cry from some later twentieth-century offerings.

This view of the eastern end of the High Street, looking eastwards, is typical of turn-of-the-century photographs in showing people standing around in the street and a lack of traffic. On the left it will be seen that the Devonia cinema is yet to come and that outside the shop is a baker's delivery cart. Possibly this belongs to Harris, and may be one of those shown on page 123. Further on, with its pillared porch, is Monkton House, at that time the private residence of the Revd H. K. Venn, the vicar of Monkton (where no vicarage existed). The first building on the right later became a lace shop (p. 55) and farther up the street may be seen one of the magnificent trees which still grace the Congregational church. The blob in the sky is not a balloon but a deterioration mark of a type liable to be found on old photographic prints; more may be seen on page 38.

In the nineteenth century the Dolphin not only supplied accommodation and refreshment for travellers but also Assembly Rooms for the town. Many events took place here, including, in the 1890s, a lecture on the Channel Tunnel.

In days when cameras were less common and were often large objects on a tripod they tended to excite interest, especially from children. The boys all seem to be watching the camera but the young lady evidently thinks something else is more interesting.

These two views of the centre of High Street in the 1930s show some changes from nineteenth-century views. An obvious innovation is the motor car, though the density of traffic had not reached the levels which made Honiton traffic jams famous in post-war years. Among changes to be seen are the introduction of the pedestrian crossing, the departure of the Banfield family from the Dolphin and the demise of the Assembly Rooms.

The Angel is one of Honiton's longest-surviving hotels—it is known to have been in existence in 1605. In 1832 it passed to William Lee, when it became Lee's Angel Hotel, and it was advertised as a stop for coaches to London, Bath and Bristol. William's widow, Elizabeth, diversified the business and in 1856 she also ran here a butcher's establishment and an Inland Revenue office. This diversification continued: in the 1930s under R.D. Sprake it was hotel, garage and the town's fire station. The Angel, however, could not rival the historic connections of the Dolphin, for it was outside here on 14 November 1688 that Lord Cornbury with a force of cavalry deserted from King James II and joined the Prince of Orange's army. James later wrote that this was the crucial turning point in his fortunes. It opened the way for the Prince to march eastwards towards London and he spent the night of the 21st and 22nd at the 'Dolfyn inn' while his secretary lodged with a hat seller named Hugh Baker, two doors away. One may wonder if this peaceful scene stayed that way, for the two dogs on the left appear to be lining up for a fight.

At first sight these two pictures, issued as picture postcards before and after the First World War, suggest an era of stability: apart from minor embellishments the buildings are essentially unchanged. The significant difference is the vehicles shown, which indicate the change in the first half of the twentieth century from the leisurely horse to hectic mechanical horsepower.

This pair of pictures, like those on page 29, also show the changing scene. In the upper one a horse vehicle half blocks the road near New Street, whereas in the lower one a car advances on the policeman on point duty, while the sides of the street are littered with parked cars. On the right a newcomer to street signs has appeared: 'Garage'.

Before 1860 travel through Honiton was by coach or on horseback, with numerous inns catering for the wants of passengers. The arrival of the railway in that year caused a move to traffic from road to rail, but a swing back occurred in the twentieth century with the development of the motor car. This picture depicts both two- and four-seater motor cars and also single and combination motorbikes. Fuel had changed from oats for horses, through coal for steam engines, to petrol for internal combustion engines and the presence of garages on both sides of the street shows the extent to which the new form of travel had developed. The unreliability of early motor cars—'a squirrel in each tool kit to run behind and pick up the nuts'—is illustrated by the large REPAIRS notice outside Moor's garage. Not all the new travelling public could afford hotel prices and the bed-and-breakfast industry developed. It will be seen that the shop next to Moor's offers good accommodation for tourists. Another growing amenity of the time is evident: the telephone, with the wires carried on telephone poles along the street. These have long since been replaced by underground cables.

Motor enthusiasts may care to identify the models shown here and compare them with those in the previous picture. Both pictures show the River Crystal, which was a striking feature of the High Street in days gone by, having been remarked on by a number of travellers. It emerged from an iron pipe opposite Marwood House and was carried in an iron trough along the pavement on the south side of the street, eventually falling into the Giseage at the bottom end of the town. There were dipping tanks at intervals from which inhabitants could obtain clean water. This was certainly more wholesome than that obtained from sundry wells, which tended to be situated near cesspits. The Crystal is, alas, no more, having been removed in a street 'improvement' scheme, though a few of the original troughs are still in position at the west end where they can be recognized by the name of the Honiton ironfounders who made them—Mickelburgh. Plans for reinstatement exist.

At the west end of the High Street, before the road drops down into the Giseage valley, there is an imposing double-fronted building seen right-centre in this photograph. It has been suggested that part of the structure is the remains of the town house of the abbots of Dunkeswell but there is no evidence to support this theory and it is unlikely that the abbots had a town house in Honiton. For many years the building was the Golden Lion, which was described by the Dean of Exeter in a letter written in 1767 as 'a bad inn'. Perhaps he was right, for on 15 May 1790 a fire broke out in the stables and no less than twenty-six horses were burned to death. In 1835 the inn was visited by Charles Dickens, then a reporter on the staff of the *Morning Chronicle*. It ceased trading as an inn in 1851 but unfortunately its sign, which showed a very spirited lion holding a ball, has not survived. The building was renamed the Manor House for no discernible reason, since it had no known connection with the manor of Honiton, and was let out in rooms. It has recently been extensively restored and is used for offices.

This view of the western High Street concentrates on the north side from the Assembly Rooms to the Manor House. Comparison with photographs taken in 1856 and with the current scene shows how little change has taken place.

In contrast this later view concentrates on the south side. It may be noted that Moor's garage is now flanked by a snack bar, perhaps aimed at the busy motorist with little time to spare to reach his holiday destination.

In moving down to the Giseage the earlier photograph again concentrates on the north side. From Dowell Street one may note the Globe Inn on the corner, the Volunteer with its thatched roof farther down and, lying back between them, the old police station.

The same scene concentrates on the south side with its telephone posts. The attempt to fit horizontal buildings to a steep slope has resulted in some strange alignments of structure, which can best be studied on the ground today.

This photograph, taken from a similar viewpoint to the top picture on page 35, illustrates various changes that took place in the first half of the twentieth century. Immediately on the right is a gap where the old police station stood; the new one is set back, an architectural feature alien to the character of the town. Beyond this is the Volunteer, with a piece lopped off to make way for a vehicle entrance to the rear of the police station. Farther down the road is the new Devonia cinema, built in an unmistakable 1930s cinema style. Like many cinemas it failed to withstand competition from television and is now an auction room and estate agency. On the left the Crystal can be seen descending towards the Giseage. This was the scene of a local field of battle on the occasion of the parliamentary election of 1763. One of the candidates was Mr Anthony Bacon who was reputed to be in favour of the recently introduced cider tax, a topic bound to cause strong feeling in Devon where cider was the staple drink. Many country people came into town and a riot ensued. Tradition has it that the gutters in High Street ran with blood and that even the water in the Giseage was tinged pink. Perhaps the bloodshed was not in vain, for the other candidate, Sir George Yonge, made representations to the government and ultimately secured the repeal of the tax.

A loaded wagon is crossing the Giseage Bridge—possibly the driver is looking thirstily at the old Anchor Inn! To the confusion of historians there were two Anchor Inns in this vicinity, though not at the same time.

These handsome iron gates led to the rectory. However the gates, rectory and tree were swept away in a post-war development of flats.

This approach to the town from the west has been seen by vast numbers of travellers over the centuries but perhaps the most unusual was Lord Cochrane, the famous sailor, who passed through Honiton in 1806 on his way to London. He had ambitions to enter Parliament and secured nomination as a candidate for the town. He gave no bribes and, as was to be expected in a corrupt age, came bottom of the poll. However afterwards he gave £10 to each of the few electors who had voted for him and stood again at the next election. Once more he gave no bribes but was elected. However, he gave no post-election payments so his supporters treated themselves to an expensive dinner and sent him the bill. His lawyers advised him to pay up, which he did, but never stood for Honiton again, complaining that the electors were corrupt. An earlier traveller was an Italian visitor, Joseph Baretti, who recorded that a short way from the town centre he saw a ducking stool. Since this is the only known reference to such an engine (as Baretti called it) it may have been in a less public spot than the Giseage, which in any case would hardly have had sufficient depth of water. Nevertheless his description indicates that the engine was on the Exeter road.

The westward expansion of the town along the Exeter road has now absorbed the originally isolated settlement of St Margaret's. Its origin is unknown but its isolated situation is explained by the earliest surviving reference, namely a grant by Bishop Brantyngham on 17 September 1374, of twenty days' indulgence to anyone who contributed to the upkeep of the pauper leper hospital of St Margaret of Honiton. As is liable to happen with such institutions, it fell on bad times but was refounded and rebuilt in about 1530 as an almshouse by Thomas Chard. Most books identify this man as Thomas Chard the last Abbot of Ford, but there is good reason to suppose that it was his namesake the Prior of Montecute, who was also Bishop of Solubria in Turkey. The buildings are no longer used as almshouses and have been divided into private residences.

St Margaret's almshouses included a chapel, seen here on the right. J. Davidson in his Church Notes, East of Devon, describes the establishment and chapel as he saw it on 22 September 1829 when there were three men and six women in residence. The oldest man had the title of governor and was due to reach the age of 90 the next Christmas. Prayers were read in the chapel on Wednesdays and Fridays by the governor assisted by another inmate who read the lessons. Davidson added that 'the inmates attend sermon and the sacrament at Honiton church, nearly 2 miles off, a great distance for these aged and infirm people'. This seems to have been a considerable imposition on these old folk and, in view of the fact that St Margaret's chapel was equipped for services, it is difficult to understand why the rector did not regard the circumstances as analogous to sickness and bring communion to the people. Perhaps it was part of the tradition of reluctance to move services from St Michael's to where the people were, a state of affairs only cured with the building of St Paul's.

Westwards from St Margaret's was the Turk's Head public house and a toll gate with a typical toll house. Of these only the latter survives. The Turk's Head was replaced by the Turk's Head Café, exterior and interior views of which are shown in these photographs. This was a product of the motor age, so ample parking space was provided.

The Saxon settlement of Honiton was in the area where St Michael's church now stands. Around 1200 the lord of the manor, following a common custom of the time, laid out a new town astride the main road, thereby attracting trade from travellers. This move left the town's place of worship on the hill, so a new street was required to connect old and new, and New Street it is to this day. Although rebuilding has resulted in some minor changes of alignments there is a view from the High Street end right up to St Michael's. A prominent feature of this photograph is the Methodist church, now council offices and a senior citizens' centre. Beside it is Chapel Street, which follows the southern boundary of the medieval new town. Other survivals of the medieval layout may be seen in Section Six, Honiton from the Air, and may be followed on the ground by pedestrians.

These two early twentieth-century views in New Street show the inevitable children 'posing' for the photographer. The wall farther up the street enclosed a property owned by Dr Jerrard, whose father and grandfather had also been medical practitioners in the town, which he bequeathed for use as a cottage hospital. Eventually it was sold and the money raised was used to build the Jerrard wing at the hospital, thus commemorating three generations of service to the people of Honiton.

This photograph, taken from the railway bridge, shows the Honiton fire brigade at work. The fact that the original print is damaged creates an atmosphere appropriate to the subject.

The original Honiton station was a fine building in brick and stone. In 1969 it was demolished in the name of improvement and replaced by a CLASP-system bungalow—a great architectural loss to the town.

W.E. Heath, who combined the occupations of photographic artist, manager of the gas works and insurance agent, was in Honiton in the second half of the 1850s. A number of photographs from this period, including this one, survive in Allhallows Museum and it seems probable that they are Heath's work. This one shows an early railway accident on the embankment to the west of Honiton station, with a number of officials wondering how to get the locomotive back on the rails. The line across the picture is a crack in the glass plate.

This view down Church Hill, also probably by Heath, pre-dates the arrival of the railway in 1860, as may be seen by the absence of the railway station and the presence of cottages which were demolished to make way for the bridge. The white posts, of which two sets are visible, are recorded as coffin posts. The medieval new town not only left the parish church behind on the hill but also the parish burial ground. Coffins therefore had to be carried up the hill, the pall bearers chanting psalms as they went. This laborious exercise led to a need for rests on the way, when the coffin would be placed on the coffin posts. How this was done is not recorded and not apparent.

This picture from the same viewpoint as the last shows the same two trees, but the scene has changed by the addition of the railway station and a row of houses.

On 26 March 1911 St Michael's church was extensively damaged by fire and the next day this ruin was all that remained.

The fire was discovered by the sexton on Sunday morning when he went into the church to prepare for morning service. Once inside he heard a crackling noise and realized that the roof was on fire. Leaving his wife to rescue what she could he ran into the town and called the chief of the fire brigade, who ran round to collect his men. They took the engine up to the church but found that the only water supply was a little in a ditch and their pump could not bring water from a greater distance. Meanwhile the sexton ran on to the rectory and the rector communicated with Exeter where the chief of the fire brigade was summoned from church. He mobilized his men and they took the powerful steam pump to Central Station, where it was loaded onto a truck and taken to Honiton. Here it was run to Littletown and pumped water up from the Giseage to a canvas tank in the churchyard, from which the Honiton men could fight the fire. The fire was eventually extinguished but only the tower and walls remained. A comparison of this photograph with the previous one shows that various unsafe parts of the structure were demolished, after which visitors were admitted. The building was restored but, as this picture shows, to describe it as the old medieval church as some do, is far from accurate.

Three

Honiton Markets and Industries

Although this is a late nineteenth-century picture, Honiton High Street on market days must have looked much like this over many centuries. Bill Norman's station bus may be seen outside the Dolphin.

For the town to flourish it was necessary to have main streets in good repair and in 1790 a petition was sent to parliament seeking leave to bring in a bill with the object of improving the situation. It was stated that passage through the town was very inconvenient, that the streets were badly paved, not kept clean and not lighted at night and that there were many 'Nuisances, Annoyances and Encroachments in the said Streets'. It was requested that provision be made for raising money to defray the expenses of the necessary work and for indemnifying anyone whose property was adversely affected. The matter was referred to a committee and after the usual parliamentary procedures the Honiton Paving Act was approved. The commissioners appointed under the act were empowered to raise the money by charging tolls and to erect toll houses on the roads leading into the town. The buildings concerned varied from full-scale toll houses to small huts. This photograph shows the Bramble Hill toll hut situated to deal with people and vehicles coming from the Exeter direction. The hut appears to have a chimney, so presumably there was a stove inside for use in the winter.

Copper Castle was the toll house on the Axminster road. It still survives, as a private house, as do the gates. The upper picture shows a typical example of the traffic which passed by soon after the abolition of the toll system in 1910. In the lower one time has moved on, the trees have grown and the horse has given way to the internal combustion engine.

The toll huts not only displayed the charges but were used by estate agents as an effective place for advertising, as seen in this photograph of the Cowley Road hut.

Clay suitable for making pottery exists in and around Honiton and it is possible that this manufacture could date back to prehistoric times. The earliest known record of a potter in the town appears in the churchwarden's accounts for 1643. Surviving examples of nineteenth-century pottery are utilitarian objects made from coarse earthenware. The rise of tourism led to the production of higher-quality decorated ware and this aspect was especially developed by Charles Collard, who owned the Honiton Pottery from 1918 to 1947. It is the Collard period floral decorations which most people associated with Honiton pottery, though only a little of this type is now produced. This photograph of the 1930s shows the women of the decorating shop at work–the lady standing is Charles Collard's daughter.

The pottery was hand-thrown in the traditional way and here we see a large vase on the wheel growing in the hands of the potter. It was just such a sight that inspired Jeremiah, writing more than 2,500 years ago, to pen his famous picture of God as the potter and Israel the clay in his hands.

Honiton is known worldwide for its lace, although it is many years since making a living by lacemaking was possible. The last man known to have tried was the crippled Walter Linscott seen here in about 1915; he soon found a more profitable occupation. His endeavour may have seemed somewhat eccentric, for at that time and for long before, lacemaking had been regarded as an occupation for women and girls. However he was in an old tradition, for in the seventeenth century lace was made by men, women and children.

The Honiton lace industry came into being in about 1560 and reached its heyday in the seventeenth century when it supplied the top fashion markets in London and on the continent. Its renown was such that it was imitated in France. Towards the end of the eighteenth century the fashion for light fabrics meant that the lace was largely net, with a sprinkling of floral motifs. This caught the attention of designers of machinery and eventually, in 1809, John Heathcoat produced the first satisfactory net-making machine. From then on, with later developments of machinery to make lace itself, the hand industry was doomed but, like Charles II, it took 'a long time a-dying'. During the nineteenth century and into the early twentieth century some fine pieces were made for special occasions, such as the Great Exhibition of 1851, but for the most part it was very sorry stuff turned out as cheaply as possible in an endeavour to compete with the prices made possible by machine production. Honiton lacemaking continues but for pleasure, not for profit. Honiton had seven lace shops in 1856 but these had dwindled to one by 1883. The latter continued until 1940 by when it had received royal warrants from four successive queens: Adelaide, Victoria, Alexandra and Mary. A second shop opened in 1926 and survives to this day as the Honiton Lace Shop, dealing in antique lace and other textiles. This photograph shows it in the 1920s. The premises was formerly the Rolling Pin and Chopping Knife public house.

Mrs Fowler's lace shop seen here in 1907. It was not well situated since it received full sun–she later moved to premises on the other side of the street.

The 1926 lace shop was later given a 1930s fascia. It will be seen that the improvements which eliminated the Crystal have also taken place.

The first decades of the twentieth century saw the production of many postcards depicting Honiton lace, usually not of the finest quality. Sometimes it was combined with pictorial views.

Apart from industry, Honiton was an important retail centre for the area and so there were many shops, such as Hoskin's on the corner of New Street.

This photograph of the shops opposite St Paul's and the Angel was presumably taken primarily for the benefit of Foale's, since two members of its staff are posed outside. This business is recorded as having flourished between 1897 and 1930. To the right one sees part of the handsome and ornate shop front which gave Hoskin's a distinguished appearance. To the left of centre is Dimond's, which can be seen in almost any photograph of this area since it has been in continuous business for well over a century. In 1838 D.M. Stirling in his book *Beauties of the Shore* wrote of Honiton: 'This interesting and comparatively handsome town, consisting chiefly of two spacious streets, well paved and lighted; and presenting well-built ranges of brick houses ...'. The impression of brick-built houses is not apparent today but this picture, and others in this section, illustrate the truth of Stirling's observation. It became a fashion to cover brick either with rendering or just with paint, but comparing the result with these pictures suggests that the town would have looked better had the brick not been covered.

In due course Monkton House ceased to be the residence of the vicar of Monkton and became the Highland Fling Café. Although big windows were added, the porch remained.

The East Devon Drapery Stores was another fine example of a brick front, combined with a colourful window display.

Isaac George Payne, whose shop in New Street is recorded between 1883 and 1906, is described in *White's Directory* of 1890 as tinplate worker, ironmonger, gas fitter, bellhanger, plumber, etc. This photograph suggests an even wider range of activities including the provision of shotgun cartridges, oil lamps for outdoor and indoor use, luggage, furniture, typewriters and beehives. The variety of goods on sale is typical of general stores in the nineteenth and early twentieth centuries but a study of directories shows that Honiton traders in the past had a particular tendency to combine more than one occupation. This is not unexpected in the case of related trades such as auctioneer and estate agent or gardener and seedsman. Less to be expected are Mrs Susan Dunning, who in 1856 combined staymaker and dining rooms, and John Merchant, who in 1857 combined tailoring with clock cleaning. The record for diversity is held by William Ward, who in 1889 is recorded as coal and manure merchant, borough surveyor and inspector of nuisances.

In 1897 Walter Thorn ran a temperance hotel in the High Street. The next directory, that of 1902, makes no mention of this but does list such an establishment in New Street run by Mrs Annie Webber. Mrs Webber continued for some years and then, shortly before the First World War, her hotel was taken over by Frederick Studley. After the war Studley became a furniture dealer, being joined by his son, seen here left, in the 1930s. Frederick Studley was a noted citizen of the town, serving as councillor, alderman and mayor and eventually being elected a freeman in 1958.

Honiton High Street has fortunately been spared almost entirely from the destruction and insensitive development which maimed so many towns in the post-war era. As a result the shop fronts shown above, which date from the early nineteenth century, may yet be seen, though the nature of the business has changed. The lower picture shows the shops where the first cinema was later situated, in festive guise for the coronation of King George V.

This handsome building was 'improved' in the 1930s by replacing the first-floor windows with a single metal-framed one. It has recently been restored to the form shown here, including the iron balconies which had been used as garden seats.

The photograph above gives a good impression of the south side of the High Street in Victorian days, from Harris the baker to the National Provincial Bank. In spite of alterations to the buildings the scene is still identifiable. The lower picture is of a charming shop front in New Street. The shop itself must have been a dog's paradise since everything advertised is for canine consumption.

Webber's and Dimond's celebrated the Devon County show of 1933 in fine style.

There is no solid evidence or even tradition about the origin of Honiton market but it seems likely that it originated in the early days of the new town. Details of the market are only available from the second half of the nineteenth century, when this photograph was taken, and show that the general goods part of it was situated in the central part of the High Street, then known as the Market Place. As this and other records show, the scene was a lively one with all kinds of goods on offer. One class of patrons in earlier days was the lacemakers. In the villages these people were paid by the truck system, that is in goods, often of inferior quality and often not to the full value of the work produced. The workers in Honiton were more fortunate, for Mrs Godolphin, giving evidence in 1863, stated that: 'In Honiton the work is brought in when it is done, very often on Fridays, and then paid for in ready money, and the people are thus able to buy their food and goods in the market on Saturday.'

The area eastwards of the general market specialized in cattle, as seen in this photograph and the frontispiece. The cattle were not penned or tethered but were kept from straying by minders, usually the younger male members of the seller's family, who would also be responsible for driving away any purchases. In the days of the tolls there was payment for any cattle brought into or taken from the market, the rate being 10*d* per twenty cattle. There is a tradition that one farmer, who objected to paying tolls, discovered that legally the bed of the Giseage was a right of way, but of course there was no toll gate on it. He therefore took his cattle in and out of town this way and by making a detour round the western side of the toll area was able to proceed to and from his farm at Awliscombe marginally the better off. It seems likely that the effort involved was not justified by the money saved and there is no tradition that this strategy was adopted by anyone else.

The area westwards of the general market specialized in sheep but these were kept in pens and only attracted half the toll charge of cattle. Sheep were an important part of the rural economy of Devon over many centuries. The number of sheep in East Devon at the time of the Domesday Survey (1087) was considerable and calculation has shown that the amount of cloth that could be made from their wool would have more than satisfied local needs. In the Middle Ages the Devon cloth industry became famous and Honiton was the third most important cloth town in the county. This industry declined in the eighteenth century, since Yorkshire, with cheap coal to produce steam power, took over production. Sheep in Devon did not die out but formed part of a general farming scene and a number of photographs of the Honiton sheep market survive from the nineteenth and early twentieth centuries, all showing scenes similar to this.

The holding of the market in the main street did not cause any inconvenience when through traffic was slight, but the shape of things to come can, with hindsight, be seen in the fact that twenty-three stage coaches passed through the town daily in 1836. It was not, however, until the increase in traffic produced by motor vehicles took place that problems began to arise. The stalls in the Market Place presented no difficulty and are still a feature today. Livestock, however, was a different matter: loose cattle and even penned sheep were found to be incompatible with motor traffic. In consequence a marketplace for livestock was created in Silver Street, with appropriate facilities and a stout perimeter wall to control any strays. This photograph shows the new market in its early days. In the foreground is the playground of Allhallows School with the old fives courts which were replaced by a classroom block in 1921. The area is now Tucker Court. On the left beyond the market are the buildings of Cowley Farm, now demolished and replaced by a car park. Beyond this again are Allhallows School playing fields with the pavilion erected in 1889. This is still extant and must count as one of Honiton's historic buildings, both on account of its age and from the fact that the man later known as 'Bomber Harris' (Marshal of the Royal Air Force, Sir Arthur Travers Harris), a freeman of the borough, played rugger from here when a schoolboy.

This is something of a mystery picture. The scene is in the Silver Street market but, with the exception of one beast, animals are conspicuous by their absence. In any case the selling took place in the middle of the market, not where this gathering is, just inside the entrance. Moreover the people assembled do not look like farmers or cattle dealers and neither the ladies nor the shop assistant with a baby are likely to be bidding for animals. It seems, therefore, that it is some kind of meeting unconnected with cattle or sheep. The solemn attitude of the men beyond the speaker may indicate a religious gathering but another possibility is that a parliamentary candidate is seeking votes.

Four

Honiton Military Affairs

Honiton has a surprisingly long military history including trainbands in the sixteenth century and a garrison in Napoleonic times. This photograph shows members of the Devonshire Regiment at the railway station.

The volunteer movement started in 1848 as a result of fears of aggression by the French and resulted in the setting up of volunteer battalions of the various county regiments. This is Sgt Russell of the Devonshire Regiment Volunteers.

This unknown volunteer is armed with a .450 Martini-Henry rifle, adopted by the British army in 1869 as the first purpose-built, breech-loading rifle.

The volunteer movement led to a demand for and the construction of many rifle ranges. One of the premier ranges in the South-West was the County Rifle Range at Honiton, more familiarly known as Roundball after the hill behind the butts. This fine twelve-target range was extended back to 1,000 yards to commemorate Queen Victoria's Diamond Jubilee in 1897, though this facility fell into disuse partly because such long-range shooting ceased to be a military requirement and partly owing to the inconvenience of shooting across a public road. The butts of a rifle range incorporate a trench in which the target mechanism is set up and from which the markers can be in safety while signalling the results of shots fired. During the building of Roundball range part of the retaining wall of the trench collapsed and this picture shows the result, with wrecked target frames and representatives of the builders wondering how to remedy the situation. In the background workmen are putting finishing touches to the stop butt, which trapped the spent bullets.

This photograph captures the spirit of a rifle range almost to perfection and, though taken on Roundball, could represent anywhere from Bisley to the humblest local range. Above the butts are the twelve target number boards and in this picture we see that targets, a little lower, are in use on ten positions. The shooters are on the 500-yard firing point but are almost invisible since they are lying on the ground in the prone position. However, as usual, various others are standing behind watching how the firers are getting on. In the left foreground a marksman is sitting, probably studying his scorebook and wondering how he could do better next time. On the right an officer is strolling away from the scene of action. As a member of Allhallows School OTC in the 1930s I often shot on this range. The first job of the markers was to erect the targets, while one of their number climbed Roundball to erect a red flag to denote that the range was being used. The first job of the firers was to herd the farmer's cows behind the firing point, though in fact none were in danger since the flight of bullets would have been well above their backs! It was a sad day for us when we heard in post-war years that this fine range had been closed for safety reasons owing to the encroachment of houses.

In days gone by the Royal Artillery used to pass through Honiton on the way to Dartmoor ranges. These troops, in about 1900, spent the night at Honiton and are here seen setting off again in the London direction, possibly making for Aldershot.

In the First World War troops from the Dominions came to join the Mother Country. There was much excitement in Honiton when a convoy of Canadian troops in motor lorries made a stop in the town.

An important contribution to the war effort was made by women in Honiton who formed a Voluntary Aid Detachment (VAD) unit of trained nurses. They are seen here with their medical officer, Dr Steele-Perkins.

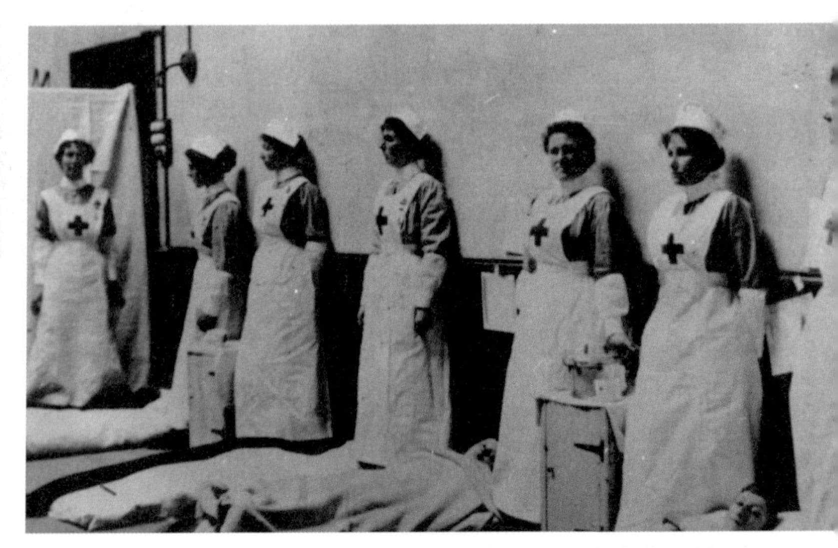

VAD training exercises took place in the Mackarness Hall, then part of Allhallows School.

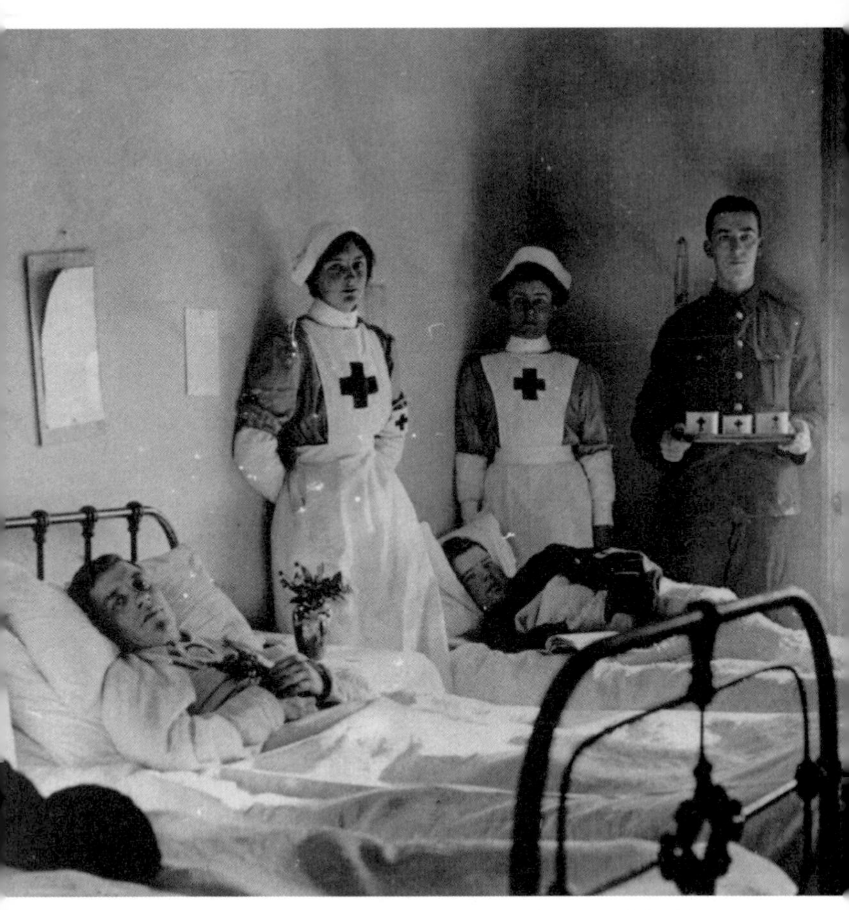

The chief activity of the VAD contingent was to run a hospital for wounded soldiers in a building immediately opposite St Paul's church. Here we see two of the men with two of their nurses and an orderly bearing mugs of tea. Nurse Pussy Cat would not be found on the staff of a modern hospital, but here she could well have had therapeutic effects by creating a homely atmosphere for men in pain and far from their homes.

As the men in the hospital improved in health they were able to move about and take their meals in the mess. Conditions were spartan, with scrubbed deal tables and enamelled iron tableware. It seems, however, that smoking was permitted.

These men had reached a stage of convalescence when they could take a drive, which must have been very pleasant for those who were not yet very mobile, as may be seen by the walking stick and crutches.

Other activities for the convalescent men included walks around the town; this picture shows two of them outside the Star. It would be nice to think that somebody has been standing them a drink.

This picture needs no extra caption.

In June 1916 Mrs Rundle and Mrs Stamp started the Honiton War Work Depot, with the aim of supplying hospitals with slippers, bandages, dressings and other medical necessities. The women were from all walks of life and wore a simple uniform of white headdress, apron and sleeves, partly for hygienic reasons and also to avoid any suggestion of class distinction. The venture was entirely self financing. One unusual item produced was moss bags, which were filled with dried sphagnum moss collected locally by school children. Dried moss will absorb up to twenty times its own weight of water and was therefore used for absorbent dressings and incontinence pads. The Depot finally closed on 30 January 1919 having produced 1,734 slippers, 13,203 bandages, etc. and 85,180 moss bags. The excess of income over expenditure amounted to £148 17s. 0d., which was given to the King's Fund for Disabled Soldiers and Sailors. Mrs Rundle noted later that the spirit of cooperation between social classes did not survive the war. Similar views were expressed in 1945 and it seems that the national unity which transcends all barriers is only possible in the face of great national crises.

An aspect of the Second World War was money-raising for aircraft production at Wings for Victory weeks. This photograph shows an RAF band marching along the High Street on such an occasion. Honiton's target of £50,000 was exceeded and £137,000 collected, sufficient to pay for two four-engined bombers.

The great citizen army of unpaid volunteers, the Home Guard, was never called upon to undertake the task it was formed for, to repel a German invasion. Nevertheless those of us who served in it were confident that we would have given invaders a hot reception.

Five

Honiton Public Events

The mayor, Mr Seabourne Hook, ready to preside at the distribution of mugs commemorating the peace celebrations of 1919.

In 1856 the Crimean War ended with the Peace of Paris and this was celebrated in great style in Honiton. The upper picture shows the High Street decorated with fir trees, flags and streamers. The town crier poses for his photograph but owing to the long exposure other people only appear as ghostly shadows. The lower picture shows Bank House decorated to an extent unequalled in any subsequent celebration.

The High Street decorations for Queen Victoria's Diamond Jubilee were on similar lines to those of 1856 but with less use of the greenery and festoons. The market stalls visible in the lower picture were used for a celebration tea in the street.

As part of the 1897 celebration a maypole was set up outside the Assembly Rooms and a team of children gave a demonstration of the traditional dance. This photograph shows the scene shortly before the dance commenced. As on subsequent occasions when an event blocked the High Street, through traffic had to use New Street, King Street and Mill Street, but pictorial evidence shows that in the period up to 1935 traffic on public celebration days was very sparse, so probably no great inconvenience was caused. Maypole dancing was not the only type of event which caused closure of the High Street for, before the advent of heavy flows of motor traffic, not only processions but also sports events were held in the street, as may be seen on page 98.

The annotation on the back of this photograph is '1897 waiting for the procession'. This animated scene gives a good impression of the pleasure and excitement of the event. The street decorations, including the fir trees, were extended right down to the Giseage and some way up Bramble Hill and these were supplemented by flags and streamers. The people to be seen vary from young children in their Sunday best through men and women of their parents' generation to the elderly lady on the right. One child has moved during the exposure and has provided a vague figure in the centre. Aspects of costume include the long white apron worn by the lady to the left, the straw hat and cane of the gentleman at left centre (a prototype for Maurice Chevalier?) and the surely unnecessary sunshade of the lady in the middle.

At the celebration for the coronation of King George V the distribution of commemorative mugs to the children took place in the forecourt of St Paul's church. The upper photograph shows the children awaiting admittance at the gates, which were subsequently removed to make way for the war memorial. The lower photograph shows the official party. This would have been the first such occasion attended by the Boy Scouts, who were inaugurated in 1908.

In 1935 the Silver Jubilee of King George V was celebrated with decorations, a procession to St Paul's church for a thanksgiving service and other events. The nineteenth-century scheme of lining the High Street with trees and adorning the buildings with greenery was not used and the emphasis was essentially on flags. Although a number of patriotic Union Jacks are in evidence the foreground string is a decidedly odd lot, but the effect is bright and cheerful.

By 1935 the pressure of traffic in the High Street caused a move in venue for the Jubilee Sports, which were transferred to Allhallows School playing field. The presentation of the commemorative mugs was also transferred here and this photograph shows the distribution in progress outside the school pavilion, with the mayor, C. N. Tweed, presiding.

This spirited photograph shows a close finish in the 1935 Jubilee Sports men's 100-yard race. There is little sign of sportswear and although one competitor has made a concession by wearing shorts, the others are content with long trousers. The winner has clearly removed his collar and tie but the third man has scorned such measures. The scene is a little reminiscent of the passage in *Tom Brown's Schooldays* in which preparations for a football match describes boys '. . . hanging up their jackets, and all who mean real work their hats, waistcoats, neck-handkerchiefs and braces, on the railings ...'. It is probable that the entrants in this race were not regular games players and did not possess sports clothes, and it must be remembered that this was an age when there was no great availability of casual wear.

While the men were competing in the 100-yard sprint the ladies were invited to compete in something less strenuous, but certainly more dextrous – the Washing Day Race. Competitors vied with each other in pegging out a standard basket of washing and the tense attitudes suggest a keen struggle. The events of the day included lunch, tea, sports, community singing and dancing. Apart from the men's sprint and the ladies' washing race there were various novelty events including skipping, wheelbarrow, egg-and-spoon and all-fours races. It was indeed a memorable day in a joyful summer which gave no hint of what was to follow in 1936.

In January 1936 the Jubilee celebrations turned to sorrow when the much-respected and well-loved King George V died. The same day his successor, Edward VIII, was proclaimed, after which there was a memorial service for King George. A procession was formed which paraded up the High Street to St Paul's church and this photograph shows various of the representative contingents entering the church. A military presence was supplied by the local Territorials and Allhallows School OTC who are about to enter the church. Also to be seen are the St John Ambulance, the Girl Guides and one member of the British Legion Band. The new reign with a young King started off with promise but before the year was out the clash between the King's personal affairs and his royal duties led to his abdication and Honiton heard its second accession proclamation within a year, the first such occurrence in the history of the town. There had been no coronation festivities since this event had been arranged to take place in 1937. New stamps had been issued during the year and after the abdication there were those who claimed that there was significance in the fact that the design placed the crown to one side and not over the King's head.

In 1937, after the abdication of King Edward VIII, a thanksgiving procession and service for the coronation of King George VI was held. The head of the procession is leaving St Paul's led by the band and representatives of the police. Behind them is the town crier and mace bearer leading the mayor, Mrs Phillips, who was then holding the office for the seventh, and by no means last, time. She is followed by the members of the Borough Council.

In 1937 coronation medals were presented to children by the mayor, Mrs Phillips, seen here with the Rector, the Revd A. Fane de Salis, and the mace bearer, John Lake.

These children are obviously enjoying the festivities—the little one would like to be on the platform too.

The Coronation Sports in 1937 included an obstacle race, seen here in progress with Allhallows Lodge in the background.

Photographs of the High Street decorated for events are quite common and one of New Street in 1937 is known. Some of the people in the latter obviously followed the photographer round to Queen Street and so we have this somewhat unexpected record.

The grandstand erected for the athletic sports on the Friday following the fair in 1883, a photograph by professional photographer A. J. Griffiths. The stand is clearly a temporary structure with a cover to give protection from the rain if the day proved wet or from the sun if the day proved to be fine. The stand is evidently facing south with the sun shining on most of the spectators and two ladies apparently found the sunlight too strong for they have opened umbrellas or parasols. In those days when ladies wore large hats it was not uncommon in a theatre to ask a lady to remove her hat so that the person behind could see the stage. On this occasion did somebody ask, 'Excuse me madam, but would you mind closing your umbrella so that I can see the races?' An interesting sartorial note is struck by the men lining the rope, who demonstrate that in the nineteenth century trousers were not worn with the back and front creases normal in the twentieth century.

The abolition of the town tolls was celebrated in June 1910 with sports events in the High Street. Could the runner visible under the flag be the winner seen on page 91?

The Devon County Show used to be held in various localities and came to Honiton in 1933. This rare event was celebrated in great style.

Honiton has had a fair since the Middle Ages. The earliest record is dated to 1221 and makes clear that at that time there was an annual fair on Allhallows Eve and Allhallows Day (1 November). It seems likely that there is some connection between this and the dedication to Allhallows of the chapel in the town centre. The date of the fair was changed in 1247, when it was transferred to the eve and feast of St Margaret (19/20 July), a date to which it has been linked ever since. The fair is opened by an event known as the glove ceremony, the significance and antiquity of which are unknown. The town crier in his official uniform of blue with a red waistcoat and tricorn hat appears in the town at noon bearing a pole ...

... which is decorated with garlands of flowers and surmounted by a large stuffed glove painted gold. He then announces the opening of the fair in these words: 'Oyez, Oyez, Oyez. The glove is up, the glove is up, the glove is up. The fair has begun, the fair has begun, the fair has begun. No man shall be arrested, no man shall be arrested, no man shall be arrested. Until the glove is taken down, until the glove is taken down, until the glove is taken down. God save the Queen.' The immunity from arrest is alleged to refer to debtors, enabling them to attend the fair freely, but like everything else associated with this ceremony, there is no contemporary evidence. The earliest known evidence for this event goes back only to the third quarter of the nineteenth century, all else is speculation. This photograph and that on the preceding page illustrates the continuity of the event in modern times, with the town crier's appearance unchanged over a period of some seventy years.

After the glove ceremony another of equally unknown origin and significance takes place. This is the hot pennies scramble. The town crier with his glove is accompanied by many children, as the photographs show. At places which have varied over the years, heated pennies are thrown from upstairs windows and the children scramble for them. This photograph shows a crowd of eager boys around 1930. The scramble may have originated as an act of charity. The heating of the pennies has been ascribed to a slightly perverse sense of humour on the part of gentry who watched the lads burning their fingers. This is quite unsupported by evidence and may well be an attempt by nineteenth-century antiquarians to find an explanation by imagination rather than research.

In the early days of cinemas the Devonia in the High Street was not Honiton's sole venue for the new 'moving pictures'. Mobile cinemas became a feature of fairs such as this one at Honiton fair in 1915, though it might not have been the draw expected, for by this time the Devonia was in operation, and many townsfolk would have seen this new novelty. Men invariably wore headgear when out of doors and an interesting variety is to be seen here—a straw boater, a uniform cap, a panama, cloth caps of various cuts and several bowlers.

At fair time the major attraction was the funfair, which took place in the fair field on the south side of King Street: the site is now occupied by Fairfield Gardens. Many showmen attended and the fair presented a gay and bustling scene with roundabouts, swings, shooting galleries and other traditional sideshows. It was patronized by many people from the town and surrounding villages, as well as by holiday visitors to the area. On one occasion I visited the fair and being in the school OTC and shooting team was attracted to a shooting range. After two shots I realized that the backsight was seriously incorrectly set and proceeded to put it right, only to be stopped by the proprietor with the order to 'let them sights alone'. My military training enabled me to 'aim off' and I won a prize, no doubt to the chagrin of the range owner. As for the error in the sights, I drew my own conclusions! Apart from the activities on the fairground various people gave performances in the street, a performer on one occasion being a dancing bear. As well as this there was a horse fair which was held in the area opposite the Volunteer.

In the eighteenth and early nineteenth centuries parliamentary elections in Honiton tended to be lively affairs with much bribery and other dubious practices going on. By the twentieth century these things were past and elections were decorous affairs. This photograph shows an orderly crowd listening to the declaration of the poll in 1936.

This photograph shows Sir Cedric Drewe, the successful candidate in 1936, acknowledging the cheers of his supporters from the balcony of the Assembly Rooms. Afterwards he drove up the High Street in an open car. I was on the pavement with some other boys, equally uninterested in politics, but we gave him a cheer. As a result he asked the headmaster to give us a special half holiday—we concluded that perhaps there was something in politics after all!

Six

Honiton From the Air

The twentieth century saw the development of air photography. This comprehensive view of the railway station would not have been possible without it.

The upper photograph, which is a remarkable technical achievement, is believed to have been taken in 1911 when the appearance of an aeroplane over the town doubtless caused a lot of interest. It must have been a notable experience for the pilot as well as enabling him to get new perspectives on the town, such as this one of St Michael's church. This view brings out the architectural structure of the building in a way quite impossible from ground level.

The advent of the aeroplane and airship led to differing reactions. Some regarded flying as just a rather silly and dangerous activity and, on the whole, military authorities saw no future in such contraptions for war. On the other hand some saw it as a revolutionary development of great potential, and history has shown that they were correct. Such people expected to see aircraft used widely but perhaps not with quite the abandon depicted in this view entitled 'Honiton in the near future'. While the airship appears to be safely above the mêlée, the density of aeroplanes at a lower altitude seems to foreshadow the later traffic problems on the ground. Heath Robinson once drew a scene on these lines and included a point-duty policeman seated on a captive balloon. Perhaps it is fortunate for the policeman on page 21 that such fancy did not become reality.

The upper photograph was taken in the early 1930s by F.S. Wakeham, a professional RAF pilot, from an altitude of 10,000 feet. The artificial rectangular layout of the medieval new town was still very much in evidence, though some development beyond it had taken place. The lower picture was taken by an amateur with an ordinary hand camera when a passenger in a two-seater plane in 1936. In spite of the indifferent quality there is a good impression of the long narrow burgage plots surviving from the medieval layout.

Like the upper photograph on the previous page this one was also taken by F.S. Wakeham, but this time from 1,000 feet. Here again the narrow burgage plots are in evidence but the fact that they were originally all the same length is obscured in the foreground because Silver Street cuts diagonally across some sixty of them. Features in the foreground from right to left include Cowley Farm, the cattle market, the playground and classrooms of Allhallows School, and Dodd's yard. On the other side of Silver Street easily recognized features are Northcote Lane, the Angel yard, the Mackarness Hall, St Paul's church and Allhallows chapel. On the south side of the High Street the Black Lion may be seen on the corner of New Street. The dark streak on the right of the picture is due to one of the wires which connected the two wings of the aircraft.

Among subjects chosen for aerial photography and reproduction as picture postcards were schools, as shown in these pictures. The Allhallows School buildings were scattered in the town centre and run across the picture from the OTC hut at top left to New Buildings at bottom right. The National School in King Street, having been built as an entity in 1861, is, in contrast, a single compact building. The Silver Street buildings of Allhallows School show that the upper photograph was taken between 1921 and 1928, and the lower one is probably from the same period.

Seven

Honiton People

A meet outside the Dolphin in about 1910.

Sir John Kennaway Bt was member of parliament for the Honiton division from 1870 to 1910, the longest period for any representative, either of the county division or of the previous borough constituency. He took an interest in the ailing lace industry and in 1887 was responsible for the appointment of a parliamentary commissioner, A. S. Cole, to make a detailed survey, which resulted in local education authority classes being established.

Sir John Kennaway was succeeded as Honiton's member of parliament by Sir Clive Morrison-Bell, who served from 1910 to 1931. This was a fraught period which saw the First World War of 1914–18, the General Strike of 1926 and the economic crisis which started in 1929, so he had to carry considerable responsibilities.

The gentleman on the right is not in fact the rector of Honiton but Sammy Bennett in fancy dress! The picture is entitled 'Carnival Curate' and the collecting box bears the legend Devon and Exeter Hospital, leading to the belief that he collected for this institution on the occasion of the Honiton Carnival. This event usually takes place in October and has grown to become one of the major such events in the area. The lower picture is of Fred Godfrey and the town fire engine. It is dateable to the Second World War since the headlamps are fitted with blackout devices.

A frustrating feature of the work of a museum curator responsible for collections of old photographs is the large number which bear neither date nor subject name. People concerned with family photographs, whether individual portraits or groups, know who they are and seldom annotate them with date or name. However, when a senior member passes on the family can well inherit potentially interesting photographs that have lost much of their significance because nobody knows the identity of the subject(s). Are your family photographs endorsed so that future generations can get full benefit from them? This picture is an example of this weakness since the print is unaccompanied by any information.

In former times the Giseage was the power house of industrial Honiton though now only one non-working water mill survives. This is the Mill House in Mill Street, which was owned by Daniel Brock in 1910. This picture shows the family group outside the front door when the decorations for the celebrations of the coronation of King George V, which took place in 1911, were much in evidence.

There is confusion in English, but not other languages, between the terms chemist and pharmacist. Strictly speaking a chemist deals with all substances but the pharmacist is a specialist in pharmaceutical preparations. In the past pharmacists had to carry out many chemical operations to prepare their formulations and so had substantial laboratories, such as that of Dyer's seen here. The pharmacist is Ted Holton.

Tom Mansfield, seen here in characteristic pose with the inevitable cigarette, was a carpenter of the old school—perhaps literally, for in the 1930s he was the Allhallows School carpenter. Many boys who went through the school in that era remember Sgt Major Aggar with affection and as many will also remember the friendly presence of Tom.

Many Honitonians went off to serve their country in the armed services in the First World War. These included Frederick Studley, seen here with a comrade in the uniform of the RFC.

Fred Jeanes was what is often described as a character. He worked, intermittently, at Honiton Pottery and had the reputation of being a fast and excellent workman. However, when he had earned some money he would go off and not be seen again for a while. When his money ran out he would reappear, but his behaviour was excused on account of his skills. He is seen here in characteristic pose.

The expense of painted portraits made them essentially the preserve of the well-to-do but the development of photography made portraiture available to those of modest means. In Honiton, Alfred John Griffiths worked as a photographer between 1883 and 1923 and these two depictions of young gentlemen of the town come from a collection of his work.

Apart from the young gentlemen, Griffiths produced portraits of other types such as these studies of a young married couple, and a mother and child.

These two pictures emphasize a contrast in personal transport. The upper one, taken on Giseage Bridge at the time of the horse fair, shows a prospective purchaser examining points. The lower one shows C.G.A. Bartlett, land agent, valuer and auctioneer, setting off down Church Hill with Mrs Bartlett on 2 June 1927. The car was known in the family as The Beetle.

Street musicians have been seen all down the ages but this one at fair time in the 1930s must be one of the most original.

Humans were not the only passengers to use Honiton station. Here R.J. Bowden gets his cart ready while a member of the station staff restrains an apprehensive prospective occupant.

The town crier had a deputy to deal with announcements if he was not available. This deputy, Walt Summers, is seen in action complete with bell and bicycle for the more rapid dissemination of the message.

The modern chimney sweep is equipped with modern technology by way of motor van, vacuum cleaner, etc. Formerly the sweep would arrive on foot, with his brush on his shoulder and a sack for the soot, as W. Rattenbury is doing here.

Mr Harris, whose shop is seen on page 63, provided services for his customers in more than one way. Bread was delivered in handcarts by lads, such as those above, using bread baskets to bring it to the door. Sometimes Mr Harris encountered poor lacemakers and he allowed them to pay in lace motifs which he did not, however, sell on—he eventually had enough for a family wedding veil. He was also a keen apiarist and was able to supply his shop with honey.

Allhallows School swimming baths was originally a roped-off area of the river at the bottom of what is now known as School Lane. In 1912 this was superseded by a swimming bath in Northcote Lane which seems very small by today's standards, but was an enormous improvement over a piece of river. Competitions became possible and here we see a competitor landing his haul of plates in the plate-diving event on 29 July 1935.

Although the bath was modest in size it was possible to hold races with four lanes. This picture shows a tense moment in the inter-house relay in the same year.

Teddy Stapleforth prepares to descend Church Hill, 1927. The windscreen is a novel feature and would, presumably, have ensured that his trilby hat did not blow off.

The Honiton Co-op String Band were a lively lot and we can imagine them giving spirited renderings of such favourites as 'Alexander's Ragtime Band' as well as the popular melodies of the wartime years.

In the nineteenth and early twentieth centuries there was a Rational Movement in medicine and dress, but there is no known evidence that a Honiton Rational Hospital actually came into being.

After the disastrous demonstration of the inadequacy of the town fire engine at the St Michael's fire, a new powerful steam appliance was purchased. It is seen here outside St Paul's church, where a demonstration of its capabilities was given by the crew.

School photographs exist in quantity and this is a typical late nineteenth-century specimen. It shows Allhallows School moderns (i.e. no Latin and Greek) with their form master.

This scene from a production of *The Pirates of Penzance* in 1935 does not have a single female player in it. All are played by Allhallows boys since the school was not a mixed one in those days. Many boys' schools had to adopt the same expedient.

This group was photographed in 1903 at Charles Turner's carpentry and joinery works situated at No. 239 High Street. The building just visible in the top left background is part of Town Dairy which was owned by William Slugget, cattle dealer and dairyman. The men in the photograph are, left to right: Alf Woodrow, Jack Critland, Bill Woodrow, William Power, Ernest Gould, Bert Rapsey, Walt Rapsey, Bill Chown.

The shopowners' cricket team of 1936 is seen here in front of the Allhallows pavilion with the umpires, Johnny Roderigo (left) and Mr Hussey, the school attendance officer (right). The team members are, left to right standing: Lewis Pavey (grocer), John Durbin (Cowley Farm), Reg Dommet (butcher), George Basset (grocer), Jimmy Hussey (estate agent), Harry Agger (Sgt Major, Allhallows School). Left to right, seated: Harold Carnell (schoolmaster and organist), Jack Sanson (cycles), E.J. Deneslow (stationer), Percy Warren (tobacconist), Frank Harding (outfitter).

This Edwardian postcard was intended for sale to holiday visitors; the pictures in this book may help you to decide whether it portrays typical Honitonians of the period.

This amazing collage of Honiton faces, with the mayor at the centre, was prepared to cheer up a sick person; it must have given hours of pleasure.

Eight

The Villages

In this photograph the Greyhound at Fenny Bridges conjures up the impression of what visitors expect of Devon villages: pub, white walls with black skirt and thatched roof, not to mention local characters.

In considering the villages that should be included in this book it is first necessary to define the extent of the Otter valley. The river cuts through the Blackdown Hills and emerges on the western side, after which it turns south through different country to the sea. It is convenient, therefore, to consider the Blackdown section as that associated with Honiton. Following down the valley we shall look at Upottery, Luppitt, Rawridge, Monkton, Combe Raleigh, Awliscombe, Weston, Buckerell, Gittisham, Payhembury, Feniton, Fenny Bridges, Fairmile and Ottery St Mary, with a glance onto the hills on each side to Dunkeswell and Bishops Tower. Upottery's most famous resident was Henry Addington, Speaker of the House of Commons, Prime Minister 1801–4 and later the first Viscount Sidmouth. He and his successor set about improving the estate and provided the village school seen above.

It is one of the glories of the Otter valley that apart from Honiton town's twentieth-century expansion and to a lesser extent Ottery St Mary's, little has changed and the beauty remarked on by travellers such as Burritt has been preserved. A consequence of this is that photographs of the villages taken seventy or more years ago look little different from modern views. Some things do change, however—for example the Upottery transport seen in the lower photograph. The outside of the church is little changed since medieval times but the interior, alas, was the subject of much ill-advised nineteenth-century 'restoration'.

The great Devonian historian and lover of the landscape, Professor W. G. Hoskins, describes Luppitt thus: 'Luppitt is a country of deep, winding lanes running from one ancient farmstead to another, haunted by buzzards in the valleys and by curlews on the heaths above, and full of flowers.' This was written in 1954 but could describe Luppitt today, or when these photographs were taken in the 1920s.

History has not dealt too kindly with Rawridge for at the time of the Domesday Survey in 1087 it was a district manor. Many manors developed into villages and even towns but Rawridge remains a hamlet, though an attractive one whether seen today or in these photographs from the 1920s.

These two views of Monkton suggest a remote rural hamlet rather than a scene on the main London road from Honiton. Careful comparison with today's scene shows that the buildings remain but that the road has been widened with the loss of many trees and hedges. The church, which is not much visited because of its position on the main road, contains some interesting stained glass by Sir Edward Burne-Jones.

The road from Honiton over Langford Bridge (above) leads to a crossroads where a left turn takes one into Combe Raleigh, the settlement in Raleigh's valley. A few houses have been added to those in this 1920s view, but the character is unchanged.

The upper photograph of Combe Raleigh rectory was offered as a picture postcard in the 1920s, but who would have been likely to have bought it save the rector and his guests? His church (lower photograph) has not changed in structure but has visually. It used to be common for churches and other old buildings to be covered with ivy and creeper but nowadays this practice is considered to cause structural deterioration and church walls are bare stone.

At the top of Honiton Hill, commanding a wide view of the Otter valley, stands Bishop's Tower, which was erected in 1843 by Bishop Copleston, one of the Coplestons of Offwell. Various speculations about reasons for building it have appeared in print but it is now known that it was simply to take advantage of the extensive views obtainable from the top. When originally constructed there was an elaborate top structure as shown in the upper photograph from about 1860. Later this was simplified to the railings which are still there today (*below*). Unfortunately this interesting folly is showing significant signs of decay of the stonework.

Awliscombe church, being set some 100 yards up a side lane, has been unaffected by the fact that the road through the village has become a busy feeder road to the M5 motorway. Therefore, though the view of the church is much the same as today, the houses in the village street are liable to be dwarfed by an enormous articulated lorry.

In this view of Awliscombe village street the people, as so often, are standing looking to see what the photographer is doing. The pigs, however, have something much more interesting than photography to engage their attention!

This picture, taken near the Weston turning on the Exeter road, shows how much like rural lanes main roads were before the advent of motor traffic.

Weston, in days gone by, was Waringstone, thus showing that it was not the farm to the west of Honiton as might be supposed, but the farm of a man named Warin who is recorded in the Domesday Survey as having a manor in Ottery St Mary.

This view of Weston 'town centre' shows a feature common in the cottages of the Otter valley: the use of random flint stone for the walls and the more easily manipulated, but more expensive, brick for the chimneys.

The approach to Weston over the river bridge changed somewhat during the first half of the twentieth century because of the modernization of the Otter Inn, as these two photographs show. As with many village pubs, changing times led to some decay in local trade, mainly in cider, with a consequent need to attempt to attract new custom from holiday-makers and families.

This photograph of Buckerell church shows that not every church was covered in ivy and creeper in the early twentieth century.

Buckerell village is overlooked by Buckerell Knap, a hill connected by a lower ridge to Hembury Fort. Past speculation has identified these features with the lost Roman station of Muridunum but not a shred of evidence has been found to support such an idea.

Dunkeswell is situated above the valley on the flat ground of the plateau near the point where the spurs which constitute St Cyres and Hembury Fort meet. The configuration of the ground led to the development of a wartime airfield which is still in use for light civil aircraft. Dunkeswell Abbey was situated beyond the village and tradition, though no evidence, associates the Abbot of Dunkeswell with Honiton (p. 33).

This view of the approach to Dunkeswell remains much the same, but beyond the end of the road and behind the photographer there are late twentieth-century developments which have not met with universal approval.

Combe House, set in a secluded site near Gittisham, is an early seventeenth-century structure which was for many years the seat of the Putt family. Since this picture was taken it has become a hotel but all its features have been carefully preserved.

This view of Gittisham church shows that it formerly had a particularly luxuriant coating of creeper which was probably more beneficial to wildlife than to the structure of the building.

Sub-post offices in small villages have declined, sometimes for want of a postmaster and sometimes because of inadequate patronage. The Gittisham post office was an imposing structure.

Gittisham is a picturesque village with an exceptionally high proportion of old houses so that it has now been designated a conservation area. The justification for this can be seen in this pair of views, one summer and one winter. The schoolgirls in their pinafores add a delightful touch to the winter scene.

Moving farther down the summer scene we encounter, in the distance, more schoolchildren, this time a mixed party with an adult. Behind the village the hill rises to the level plateau and although nowadays known as Gittisham Hill, its older name was Bromdun, meaning the hill covered with broom. This part of the plateau, stretching on to Farway common, contains the largest Bronze Age cemetery in Devon apart from on Dartmoor.

These two picture postcards of Payhembury of unknown date resemble a 'spot the difference' competition. It is obvious that the lower one is later since it includes a better surfaced road with a car on it. It probably dates from about 1930. Other differences include the removal of creeper from the house on the left and a change of pattern of pedestrian tracks on the rough ground. Readers should be able to spot other differences.

Fenny Bridges tended to be a halting place for travellers and motor coaches, as seen in this photograph. The scene, however, was not always so peaceful for a desperate battle took place here in 1549 and this had an important impact on national affairs. In that year the Book of Common Prayer was issued and ordered to be used in place of the old services. Many people in Devon and Cornwall did not approve. Eventually a fight started at Sampford Courtenay which soon became a full-scale rebellion. Exeter was besieged and the rebel army advanced to Fenny Bridges. Lord Russel was in charge of a small government force at Honiton and was, in the words of the contemporary historian John Vowell, 'daily waiting and looking for the promised Help and Supply, which came not, he was in an Agony, and of heavy Cheer'. However, help did eventually arrive and Russel marched against the rebels and succeeded in capturing the bridge. 'And having recovered the Bridge and the River, all the Rebels (such as were escaped) were gathered in a Meadow near adjoining in the lower side of the Bridge; upon whom they so fiercely followed, and gave the Ouset, that though, not without good Store of Blows and Bloodshed they, in the End, gave the Enemy the Overthrow, and had the Upper-hand.' This was the turning point and the rebellion was soon put down.

The Bloomfield guest house is an example of an alternative for travellers who did not wish to patronize hotels or inns. Apart from accommodation and fruit, lunches and, inevitably, cream teas were available.

Fenny Bridges was not just a spot on a rather noisy main road, as this peaceful scene shows.

Feniton church is notable for its memorial to Bishop Patterson who died a martyr in the South Seas in 1871. This attractive view of the building is enhanced by the pinafored schoolgirls.

In this village scene a number of inhabitants, and the horse, have stopped to see what the photographer is up to.

Time has moved on in Feniton to about 1930 as may be seen by the car and the lady's hemline. No doubt the bike is a prized possession.

The Fairmile Inn on the main road presents a peaceful scene in this photograph in which the horse and leg power are the engines of locomotion.

This view of the Fairmile Inn contrasts with that on the previous page: the motor era has started. Leaning against the post office wall there is a powerful motorcycle and to the right are two RAC patrolmen. Also to be seen is a RAC scout's motorcycle combination with its box-like sidecar containing emergency equipment. In all probability Fairmile, which was referred to as 'le faire mile' in about 1425, derives its name from the fact that here there was a particularly good stretch of road. In the sixteenth century Devon roads were notoriously bad, as shown by Risdon's oft quoted remark: 'Rough and unpleasant to strangers travelling those ways, which are cumbersome and uneven, amongst rocks and stones, painful for man and horse.' In 1688 William Prince of Orange encountered conditions such as these on his march from his landing place at Brixham to Exeter. However, in 1695 Celia Fiennes wrote that 'From Exeter I went to Honiton, 15 miles, all fine gravel way, the best road I have met with in all the west.' So, it may be that Fairmile was justly named.

On the road from Fairmile to Ottery St Mary one passes the late sixteenth-century house of Cadhay. The state of excellent preservation makes dating of old photographs almost impossible and this 1930s picture could be quite recent.

A mill leat taken from the Otter not far from Cadhay served a serge factory and gave rise to one of Ottery St Mary's sights, the unusual tumbling weir through which surplus water finds its way back to the river.

Ottery St Mary, a small town rather than a village, has since medieval times been second only in importance in the valley to Honiton. A fundamental difference between the two settlements is that Honiton has the planned new town layout, whereas Ottery has just grown, leading to twisting streets and a more compact, almost circular shape. In the great days of the cloth trade it was a noted place and when the lace industry developed it became an important centre. In 1698, when Honiton had 1,341 lacemakers, Ottery had 880, substantially more than any other place in the area. Ottery St Mary was a market town and in older records the square in the middle now called Broad Street is referred to as the Market Place. Like Honiton, Ottery has been spared the demolition and unsympathetic redevelopment so common in the mid-twentieth century, so that this early twentieth-century photograph of the town centre is little different from the same view today.

This view over the rooftops leads the eye to Ottery's most famous feature, St Mary's church, one of the glories of Devon. Bishop Grandisson established a collegiate foundation here in 1337 and set about creating a collegiate church on a grand scale, though how much of the previous church building was incorporated is not known and is a matter for debate. The church is like a cathedral in miniature and, indeed, the plan with two transept towers must have had its inspiration in Exeter Cathedral. Though Honiton is by far the most important place in the Otter valley, the church at Ottery St Mary is by far the most important building. It is therefore a fitting subject to conclude this survey of Honiton and the Otter valley in old photographs, but leaves us to speculate on how the history of Honiton and Ottery would have differed had the good bishop decided to build his church at Honiton.

Acknowledgements

The majority of the photographs in this book have been reproduced from items in the collections of Allhallows Museum, for which, in my capacity as honorary curator, I am responsible. I am grateful to my fellow members of the management committee for their endorsement of this project. Since the museum's collecting policy limits acquisitions to items relating to the town I had to seek elsewhere for pictures of the wider context and I am most grateful to David Thomas for generously making available his extensive collection of picture postcards in Section Eight, The Villages. I am also grateful to Jonathan Page for the pictures of Weston and to Pat Perryman for 'the most boring postcard' and 'Honiton in the near future'.

Both Pat Perryman and Bill Crane have given assistance with the identification of some of the persons in Section Seven, Honiton People.

Allhallows Museum is an independent registered charity run entirely by volunteers and all royalties accruing from this book have been assigned to it.

Books on the History of Honiton

Farquharson A.S., *History of Honiton*, Exeter, 1868

Farquharson A.S., *History of Honiton*, 1891 (MS in Honiton library)

Coxhead J.R.W., *Honiton and the Vale of the Otter*, Raleigh Press, Exmouth, 1949

Yallop H.J., *Honiton in Old Picture Postcards*, European Library, Zaltbommel, 1983

Coxhead J.R.W., *Honiton, a History of the Manor and Borough*, Devon Books, Exeter, 1984

Yallop H.J., *The History of the Honiton Lace Industry*, University of Exeter Press, Exeter, 1992

Research papers on various topics relating to the town will be found in the following journals: *Proceedings of the Devon Archaeological Society, Transactions of the Devonshire Association, Devon Historian, Devon and Cornwall Notes and Queries.*

At the end of the First World War many relics were distributed around the country and village greens were 'decorated' with tanks. Another favourite item was a captured German gun like this one presented to Honiton, where it remained until taken for scrap in the Second World War.